GROUND BREAKERS
BLACK MOVIE MAKERS
SPIKE LEE

by Joyce Markovics
and Alrick A. Brown

CHERRY LAKE PRESS
cherrylakepublishing.com

CHERRY LAKE PRESS

Published in the United States of America by Cherry Lake Publishing Group
Ann Arbor, Michigan
www.cherrylakepublishing.com

Reading Adviser: Beth Walker Gambro, MS, Ed., Reading Consultant, Yorkville, IL
Content Adviser: Alrick A. Brown, Film Professor and Filmmaker
Book Designer: Ed Morgan

Photo Credits: David Shankbone/Wikimedia Commons, cover and title page; © Andrea Raffin/Shutterstock, 5; William P. Gottlieb/Ira and Leonore S. Gershwin Fund Collection, Music Division, Library of Congress, 7; freepik.com, 8; Wikimedia Commons, 9; Thomson200/Wikimedia Commons, 10; © Sean McNeil/TNS/Newscom, 11; Public Domain, 12; Wikimedia Commons, 13; © UNIVERSAL PICTURES/Album/Newscom, 14; David Shankbone/Wikimedia Commons, 15; © UNIVERSAL PICTURES/Album/Newscom, 16; Wikimedia Commons, 18; Wikimedia Commons, 19; © JIM RUYMEN/UPI/Newscom, 21.

Library of Congress Cataloging-in-Publication Data

Names: Markovics, Joyce L., author. | Brown, Alrick, author.
Title: Spike Lee / by Joyce Markovics and Alrick A. Brown.
Description: Ann Arbor, Michigan : Cherry Lake Publishing, [2023] | Series: Groundbreakers: Black moviemakers | Includes bibliographical references and index. | Audience: Grades 4-6
Identifiers: LCCN 2022039662 (print) | LCCN 2022039663 (ebook) | ISBN 9781668919774 (hardcover) | ISBN 9781668920794 (paperback) | ISBN 9781668923450 (adobe pdf) | ISBN 9781668922125 (ebook) | ISBN 9781668924785 (kindle edition) | ISBN 9781668926116 (epub)
Subjects: LCSH: Lee, Spike—Juvenile literature. | Motion picture producers and directors—United States—Biography—Juvenile literature. | African American motion picture producers and directors—Biography—Juvenile literature. | CYAC: African Americans—Biography.
Classification: LCC PN1998.3.L44 M27 2023 (print) | LCC PN1998.3.L44 (ebook) | DDC 791.4302/33092 [B]—dc23/eng/20220919
LC record available at https://lccn.loc.gov/2022039662
LC ebook record available at https://lccn.loc.gov/2022039663

CONTENTS

THIS IS SPIKE

"YOU'VE GOT TO HAVE HEART AND YOU'VE GOT TO HAVE DRIVE. AND WHEN YOU GET KNOCKED DOWN, YOU'VE GOT TO PICK YOURSELF UP."

—SPIKE LEE

Filmmaker Spike Lee lives by these words. For almost four decades, he has been hard at work making movies. Spike's more than 30 films not only tell great stories, they tackle big issues. These issues include race and **injustice**. His movies urge people to watch, listen, and, most importantly, to think. On top of that, Spike teaches and supports the next **generation** of filmmakers of color.

Every Spike Lee movie ends the same way. The following phrases appear on the screen: "By Any Means Necessary," "Ya' Dig?," and "Sho Nuff."

EARLY LIFE

On March 20, 1957, Shelton Jackson Lee was born in Atlanta, Georgia. His mother, Jacqueline, was a teacher, and his dad, Bill, was a jazz musician. When Shelton was a baby, his mom nicknamed him Spike. Why? He was fiery, tough, and resilient, even as a small child.

Spike was the oldest of three children. Jacqueline taught her children about being African American. She wanted her children to be proud of their heritage. Spike's mom also shared her love of art and movies with her kids. She often took little Spike with her to the movies.

Spike would sometimes go to clubs to hear his father play jazz. Spike's dad would go on to write music for many of his son's movies.

When Spike was 2 years old, his family moved to Brooklyn, New York. Brooklyn felt like a whole new world to Spike. The sights and sounds of Brooklyn filled his young mind with wonder. Brooklyn would later have a big impact on Spike's movies.

During his childhood, Spike's mom worked at a private school in New York City. When Spike was old enough, his parents gave him the option to choose a private or a public school. Spike chose a public school where there would be other Black kids like him. He graduated from John Dewey High School in Gravesend, Brooklyn, in 1975.

The "Key to Knowledge" statue stands in front of John Dewey High School.

After high school, Spike went to Morehouse College, a historically Black college in Atlanta. It felt like a good fit because Spike's father and grandfather had gone there. When Spike started college, he was skinny, wore thick glasses, and struggled with self-confidence. "Morehouse is where I became a man, but also, there were a lot of trials and tribulations," said Spike.

Morehouse College in Atlanta, Georgia

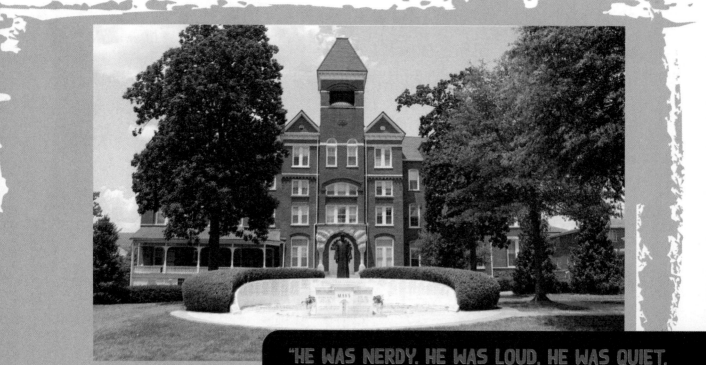

"HE WAS NERDY. HE WAS LOUD. HE WAS QUIET. HE WAS BROOKLYN. . . . SPIKE WAS SPIKE."
—ROLANDA WATTS, SPIKE'S COLLEGE FRIEND

Freshman year, Spike got C's and D's in his classes. He fought with his roommate, and he missed Brooklyn every day. During Spike's sophomore year, his mom got sick and passed away. Spike was **devastated**. He went home to Brooklyn that summer. To distract himself, Spike picked up a camera. "I started filming," he said.

When Spike returned to Morehouse in the fall, he said, "I want to make film." He had found his calling. Soon after, Spike made his first movie, *Last Hustle in Brooklyn*. One of his professors said that Spike told stories as he saw them, which made him a great storyteller. For the rest of college, Spike got straight A's.

Bedford-Stuyvesant, Brooklyn, in the late 1970s

After college, Spike enrolled at New York University (NYU) and got a **master's degree** in film and television. He made another short film at NYU called *Joe's Bed-Stuy Barbershop: We Cut Heads* in 1983. Set in Bedford-Stuyvesant, Brooklyn, the movie is about a bustling barbershop, where the main character struggles to stay true to himself while earning a living.

Joe's Bed-Stuy Barbershop: We Cut Heads won an Academy of the Motion Picture Arts and Science's Student Award.

MAKING MOVIES

Not long after graduating from film school, Spike made his first **feature-length** movie, *She's Gotta Have It*, in 1986. He shot the black-and-white movie over 12 days. Spike made the movie on a very small **budget** with help from his grandmother Zimmie and his college friends at Morehouse.

Spike Lee in 1989

She's Gotta Have It tells the story of a strong, young Black woman trying to find her way in the world. It was a huge success. The money Spike earned from the movie allowed him to start his own film production company. He called it 40 Acres and a Mule Filmworks. *School Daze,* Spike's next movie, was about a Black college much like Morehouse. In 1989, Spike made his most famous film, *Do the Right Thing*.

40 Acres and a Mule Filmworks in Brooklyn

The company name "40 Acres and a Mule Filmworks" refers to a period in American history called Reconstruction. After the Civil War (1861–1865), the U.S. government gave some formerly enslaved people a parcel of land and, sometimes, a mule. Then the government abruptly stopped the program and made the people give the land back.

Do the Right Thing takes place on a scorching summer day in a Brooklyn neighborhood, not unlike the one where Spike grew up. In the movie, Italian Americans run a pizzeria in a Black community. The movie deals head-on with race and the tense relationships between different groups of people. Spike shows all the characters' fears and frustrations, creating empathy for them.

As tensions build, violence and tragedy erupt. One of the Black characters, Radio Raheem, is killed by police for playing his radio too loud. Chaos follows. Through Spike's superb storytelling, the audience considers painful truths. The movie was a huge hit and named best movie of the year by critics.

In addition to writing, directing, and producing the movie, Spike plays Mookie, a pizza delivery man, in *Do the Right Thing*. He also hired a lot of unknown actors of color for this film and others, many of whom later became famous.

Following the success of *Do the Right Thing*, Spike went on to make dozens of other feature films. He presented stories of jazz musicians, athletes, soldiers, bank robbers, and other subjects. One of Spike's most celebrated films was a biopic about Malcolm X. He showed the civil rights leader as a great man with flaws.

A film critic called *Malcolm X* "one of the great screen biographies."

"I THINK PEOPLE WHO HAVE FAULTS ARE A LOT MORE INTERESTING THAN PEOPLE WHO ARE PERFECT."
—SPIKE LEE

More movies followed, including documentaries. Spike's *When the Levees Broke* (2006) examined the U.S. government's failure to help poor Black people affected by Hurricane Katrina. He also made a movie about a 1963 church bombing that killed four little Black girls. In 2019, after being passed over for many awards, Spike won an Academy Award for his film *BlacKkKlansman* (2018).

Spike calls all his films "A Spike Lee Joint." He uses the word *joint* to refer to a thing, so, in other words, he's saying "A Spike Lee Thing."

SPIKE'S IMPACT

For almost 40 years, Spike Lee helped change the way Black stories are told on film. He is known around the world as one of the most original and creative filmmakers working today. Spike not only writes, directs, and produces movies, he's also acted in 10 of his own films. Through his work, Spike has inspired a new generation of filmmakers and actors. When asked how long he would continue making movies, Spike said, "I got a lot more stories, a lot more films . . . a lot more work." He continued, "This is my path in life, so I'm not gonna run from it. I just wanna speak the power of the truth, and continue to tell our stories."

"WHEN YOU DO WHAT YOU LOVE, YOU LIVE LONGER. AND THAT IS NOT TIED TO MONEY. A LOT OF PEOPLE HAVE A LOT OF MONEY AND AN UNHAPPY LIFE."
—SPIKE LEE

Like his mother, Spike became a teacher. He's also a father and raised two children with his wife, Tonya Lewis. Spike also makes time to cheer on his favorite sports team, the New York Knicks.

Spike Lee and his wife, Tonya Lewis

FILMOGRAPHY

SPIKE'S FEATURE MOVIES

1986	*She's Gotta Have It*		2000	*Bamboozled*
1988	*School Daze*		2002	*25th Hour*
1989	*Do the Right Thing*		2004	*She Hates Me*
1990	*Mo' Better Blues*		2006	*Inside Man*
1991	*Jungle Fever*		2008	*Miracle at St. Anna*
1992	*Malcolm X*		2012	*Red Hook Summer*
1994	*Crooklyn*		2013	*Oldboy*
1995	*Clockers*		2014	*Da Sweet Blood of Jesus*
1996	*Girl 6* *Get on the Bus*		2015	*Chi-Raq*
1998	*He Got Game*		2018	*Pass Over* *BlacKkKlansman*
1999	*Summer of Sam*		2020	*Da 5 Bloods*

GLOSSARY

biopic (BAHY-oh-pic) a movie about a person's life

budget (BUHJ-it) an estimate of expected expenses for a given time

civil rights (SIV-uhl RITES) the rights everyone should have to freedom and equal treatment under the law, regardless of who they are

critics (KRIT-iks) people who judge or criticize something

devastated (DEV-uh-stay-tid) terribly shocked or upset

documentaries (dok-yuh-MEN-tuh-reez) movies that recreate actual events or true-life stories

dolly (DOL-ee) a small wheeled platform on which a movie camera can be mounted

empathy (EM-puh-thee) the ability to imagine another person's emotions, thoughts, or attitudes

feature-length (FEE-chur-LENGTH) full-length, such as a feature-length film

generation (jen-uh-RAY-shuhn) a group of people born around the same time

heritage (HER-i-tij) traditions that are handed down from the past

injustice (in-JUHS-tis) unfair treatment

master's degree (MAS-terz dih-GREE) a degree awarded by a graduate school for advanced study

production (pruh-DUHK-shuhn) describes a business that produces content for movies, for example

Reconstruction (ree-kuhn-STRUHK-shuhn) the rebuilding of the South after the Civil War that lasted from 1865 to 1877

resilient (ri-ZIL-yuhnt) the ability to recover after tough times

tragedy (TRAJ-uh-dee) a sad and terrible event

tribulations (trib-yuh-LEY-shuhns) difficult experiences

FIND OUT MORE

BOOKS

Blofield, Robert. *How to Make a Movie in 10 Easy Lessons*. Mission Viejo, CA: Walter Foster Publishing, 2015.

Frost, Shelley. *Kids Guide to Movie Making*. New York, NY: Amazon KDP, 2020.

Willoughby, Nick. *Digital Filmmaking for Kids*. Hoboken, NJ: John Wiley & Sons, 2015.

WEBSITES

Britannica Kids: Spike Lee
https://kids.britannica.com/students/article/Spike-Lee/312134/related#nodeId=main&page=1

State University of New York: Spike Lee
https://www.albany.edu/writers-inst/webpages4/archives/lee_spike.html

William & Mary: Spike Lee
https://www.wm.edu/news/stories/2012/lee-get-educated,-do-what-you-love-123.php

INDEX

ABOUT THE AUTHORS

Joyce Markovics has written hundreds of books for kids. Movies have helped shaped her outlook on life and inspired her to tell stories. She's grateful to all people who have beaten the odds to make great art. Joyce dedicates this book to David Tuttman, a cinematographer and director with a huge heart.

Alrick A. Brown is a storyteller and an Assistant Professor at NYU who uses filmmaking to touch the hearts and challenge the minds of his audiences. His creativity is shaped by his time living and working in West Africa, his upbringing in New Jersey, and his travels around the world.